Watering the Marigolds

Muriel Bergel

Watering the Marigolds

Watering the Marigolds
ISBN 978 1 76109 618 1
Copyright © text Muriel Bergel 2023
Cover image: Imran Arif

First published 2023 by
Ginninderra Press
PO Box 3461 Port Adelaide 5015
www.ginninderrapress.com.au

Contents

kintsugi	7
stagnant	8
grief in three parts	9
everything	10
creation	11
elpis	12
watering the marigolds	13
the dragonfly	14
messages from mum	15
goddess	16
djembe	17
the house on the avenue	18
coffee at the beach	20
breaking free	21
dancing queen	22
swiping right	23
gumtree	24
brushstrokes	25
multiverse	26
siren song	27
I knew you once	28
what the moon taught me	29
la cumparsita	*30*
a walk to the past in Leichhardt	31
lovers	32
cloud watching	33
little girl lost	34
boxes	35
refractions	36
ode to my ugg boots	37

inferno	38
life's not waiting	39
the tidal wave	41
D = ST	42
philematology	43
untamed	44
everything will be ok	45
wanderlust	46
maze	47

kintsugi

an object
desired
judged
you want to touch it
have it
make it yours
scared to hold it
it's too fragile
what if it breaks
but it's already broken
imperfect
flawed
pieced back together with gold
do you still want it
dappled beauty
reflecting what's inside
I see now
it's already mine

Kintsugi is the Japanese art of putting broken pottery pieces back together with gold, the idea being that by embracing its flaws and imperfections, it becomes more beautiful.

stagnant

lost
a detour into stillness
the road leads back
comfortable in my discomfort
I look out the window
the view is still the same
repetition is in charge
freedom succumbs
grounded
roots buried deep
I open the window
air invades my space
I breathe
uninvited but I let it stay
it knows where to go
so I follow

grief in three parts

i

the earth
crumbles beneath me
I fall
darkness envelops me like a heavy winter blanket
a familiar comfort in the dark
lost and numb
love drains from me
aching breathing disintegrating

ii

puzzle pieces scattered on the floor of my mind
some no longer fit
you were there once
I look but I cannot see
dreams no longer mine
shadows in my soul make
dandelion wishes

iii

how long have I been here?
too long?
maybe not long enough?
pain clings to me like a leech
tears dry up
salt preserves me
strength drips down like rain
touches me awakens me
opening my eyes to the light

everything

I feel you
I am you
and you are me
always here
vagabond specks floating through time
tears flowing
giving life to the gardenias
stardust party poppers
litter the streets
made to the same rhythm
atomically connected
everything is me
everything is you

creation

I ride on a boat of heaven
through the flowery pool
the golden lotus shines its light
of life through the gateway
to the jade garden

a pearl inside my oyster
an eternal gift of love summons you in
savouring the fruits of desire
ruby red seeds of creation

wrapped in my lips
moon divine I invite you
awaken the goddess
her sacred power unleashed

elpis

unseen and untouchable
yet I still cling to her
needing to feel her comforting hand
touch my spirit

lost without her
scared
I follow the white dove
that leads me to where I need to be
jumping over the concrete cracks
sprouting life as I go

forever trapped in a clay jar
wanting her to make her escape
I am dirt and dust
I am clay
the lid is forever stuck
she cannot come out

the dove sings in my ear
a familiar song
look inside
it serenades me
I am dirt and dust
I am clay

In Greek mythology, Elpis is the spirit of hope. She was trapped in a jar by Zeus and entrusted to the care of Pandora.

watering the marigolds

my garden invaded by weeds
that suffocate life
stubborn in its fortitude
it won't surrender
pulling out the weeds one by one
a crescendo sigh as I resuscitate
the soil underneath fertile
longing to be the giver of life
to reawaken from its forced slumber
planting the seeds deep into darkness
nestled in their regenerative blanket
eager to see the light
green shoots welcome the
sun's gentle kiss
as they break free
the fiery orange blooms are thirsty
I water the marigolds
quenching their golden hues
their musky scent exposed
lingering in my heart
a perpetual resurrection

the dragonfly

from the water she is born
in darkness she lives
before rising up to the light
to greet the sun
I ride on her back
an iridescent tango
reflected through her wings
carrying wisdom in her agile flight
beyond my mind she sees
fracturing illusions
as she flirts with the wind
her eyes remember
the depth of my spirit
before I do
a warrior in her power
her serenity guarding me
I am safe

messages from mum

do you want a cheese sandwich
come talk to me
shall we spa today
drinks?
drinks?
drinks?
let's go to Ikea
do you have coconut
my maple syrup has escaped
I bought you bullets
do you want soup
are you angry at me
whiskey o'clock are you coming
creme caramel available – yum
are you ready to walk
yeah!

goddess

I see her wipe the tears
now pooling at her feet
forming puddles filled
with yin and yang
the fairy floss once sweet
tastes bitter now
but she can't spit it out
it burns in her mouth

the street sign names are blank
how will she find her way home
she called me a goddess once
but she forgot she is one too
her goddess face reflected
in the puddles at her feet

she puts on her gum boots
and splashes in the light and dark
remembering the way back
she doesn't need directions
glitter spilling from her lips
as she opens her mouth
she is home

djembe

Three spirits joined together
harmoniously contained
within your curvy form
their power connecting me
across your skin my hands become
a vessel for your sacred sounds
bass
slap
tone
gather together in peace
your name demands
bass
slap
tone
I cradle you between my legs
your beat an instrument of my soul
your rhythms a celebration in my heart
bass
slap
tone
a call and response
I follow your voice

A djembe is a West African drum. It is said that the drum contains three spirits, the spirit of the tree from which it was made, the spirit of the animal whose hide was used for the drum head, and the spirit of the instrument maker.

the house on the avenue

she stands guard
proudly greeting the avenue
unaware of her potential
an unfinished melody
the scent of the past is her perfume
she remembers everything
time is a tattoo on her facade
a maternal container for life, a womb
nurturing and protective

with room for two
she watches
the lovers
as they fill her with art
politics and poetry
they lovingly tend to her every need
she stretches her arms

now with room for four
she watches
the daughters
a pit stop
safe haven on their journey
welcomed in her embrace
her staircase like a spine ascends
we take root
our saviour

now with room for five and six
she watches
returned with more
the grandchildren
secure now
she exhales
a mirror to our spirit
silent witness
to the cycle of our lives

coffee at the beach

it's been too long you say
an overdue reunion
we take off our shoes
our toes grounded in the sand
poetry and coffee
on a Friday afternoon

feeling your fear
I know it too
but not as well as you
so very well acquainted
pandora's box is open
but you want the lid back on
I tell you keep it off

your eyes see a different life
I wipe the sand off your face
you want to join the surfers
feel the water regulate your soul
don't be scared
you are water too

lying on the sand
tipping over life
a comforting embrace
you ask to kiss my lips
I remember your taste
time running through my fingers
on a Friday afternoon

breaking free

caged in monotony
a windowless room
houses my essence
is it night-time
I can't remember
a relentless slumber
overcomes me

I count the ants as they march
back and forth under my door
108
envious of their purpose
I plan my escape

In my dream
there's a horse saddled up
waiting outside
to rescue me
I used to ride once

I'm being chased
they take aim
shooting at me
I look behind
my horse bolts
galloping like my heart
as a gate opens up

I think it's morning now
my hands are cold
in my pocket I find a key
I break free

dancing queen

fairy lights are her crown
a dance floor her palace
she wears the sun and stars
around her neck
a celestial jewel

she lends you her strength
a silent soliloquy
no words are required
rhythm is her mother tongue
keep dancing my friend

mirror ball orb
adorns the royal regalia
in a gown of lunar silver
she closes her eyes
creation in motion

she dances
the foreplay to life
an anthem for her being
just one more song she says

swiping right

my hands conduct a mindless
symphony
an ear-splitting harmony
cymbals clanging
the sound draws me in

I play solitaire with unknown faces
miss out if I don't
miss out if I do
an un-winnable game

I stare blankly
passing time
time passes
I stop

my hands reach out again
No
No
No
Maybe
Yes
No

the profiles coalesce
a bleary landscape
optimism fades into lassitude
an unsatisfying paradox

gumtree

In reverence
I watch you through my window
dignified in your pose
a ladder connecting our worlds
above and below
the earth bowing down at your feet

generously feeding those that come to visit
like a noisy Sunday lunch at *abuela*'s
I hear the bees and lorikeets
at play around you
your branches call them in to eat
maternal and protective
your breath preserves us

your changing colours marking time
a hypnotic sway
as the wind salutes you
what hidden secrets lie inside

at night when it's time to sleep
a shadow puppet show
staged against my bedroom walls
recounting the story of life
here beyond my existence
will you remember me

Abuela is grandmother in Spanish.

brushstrokes

my blood forever blending
into a swirling shadow
a contrast in black
hearing a whisper saying
be the light
I am now shining
my temple erected
in an undertone of grey
diving into the boundlessness
coming up for air
my hand swipes across the canvas
a chain
holds me together
harmonious palate
shows signs of life
dotted yellow
with contours of joy
a perfect circle spirals
with splatters of pink
the little girl dreams
seeing reflections in the baubles
chords of golden threads
illuminate the still life
now in motion

multiverse

decisions fractured by time
split in two
accidental beauty
atoms colliding into
the galaxy that is you
nothingness empties into
chaos
order
renewing your indestructible soul
memories in the distance
barely touchable
are they yours
a different path taken
where does it lead
concentric circles of
creation
destruction
an impossible puzzle ball
particles of unfulfilled dreams
a jewel at each vertex

I open the door to
a different world
the vastness closes in
expanse on the other side
mistakes corrected
possibilities reaching
perfect symmetry
explosion
rebirth
we look at each other
overlapping

siren song

kneel before me she says
once forbidden
his mouth worships her
do not talk
the sirens in
the salty sea
will hear you
shhhh
come they cry out
but her song is sweeter
listen to me
your boat will crash
I will guide you to shore
shhhh

I knew you once

a time before
so familiar
two parallel lines
reminiscences
just out of reach squinting
I can barely make them out
glimpses of you
left out in the sun
the colour is fading
past evaporates
a downpour creates
sinkholes
overflowing with our lost reality
the ring gets tossed in
collision into my consciousness
an imposter
in the same disguise

what the moon taught me

a reliable friend
that always shows up
in darkness she reveals to me
the secrets to life
her celestial wonder
lustrous wisdom in the obscurity
the eye of the night
she guides me
perfectly imperfect
unconcerned she shines
her light regardless
moving through the phases
of life with grace
never still
the potentiality of new beginnings
in her face
stay grounded she says
casting shadows on the surface
of my being
together we are in sync
she tucks me in
reminding me to keep dreaming
prelude to my awakening

la cumparsita

she sat on the stool
as if it were her throne
the instrument old and off key
but priceless
monochromatic majesty
I want to remember her hands
how they moved across the piano
an allegro pace
to hear her turn each page of
the old sheet music
the scent of humidity lingering
her precious cargo
transported across the oceans
we gathered around
she played
the notes forever part of us
rhythmic comfort
tango her music
the sound of nostalgia's embrace
our pulse

La cumparsita is a tango written in 1916 by the Uruguayan musician Gerardo Matos Rodríguez.

a walk to the past in Leichhardt

I walked down your streets tonight
sentimentality on every corner
I knew you intimately once
my story shared with yours
a voyeur to my life
as it played out in front of you
recollections from a different time
an acquaintance now
through the rain I look at you
veiled tenderness envelopes me
you are different now
I am too
beginnings and endings
nothing stays the same
I want to run
but change catches up
a cord still attaches us
I have tried to cut it
but my scissors are rusty
so I keep coming back

Leichhardt is an inner-city suburb of Sydney, NSW.

lovers

an afternoon walk through the park
a sneaky kiss behind the trees
together we climb the steep staircase
its familiar to me now
I know where it leads
laughing at your squeaky bed
the sound echoing our movements
a distracting symphony
you call out my name

architecture books
black underwear and limes
twilight drinks on the porch
the taste of whiskey and
longing lingers in our mouths
like two teenagers
fumbling in the dark
searching for our lost youth
and a room
a moment forgetting life

cloud watching

come lie with me
and watch the clouds
a vehicle for immortals
in the celestial realm
what secrets lie behind
that which we cannot see
the breath of dragons
a nymph's billowing robe
holding the earth's tears
requisite for a sunset
lost in a moment of your shade
we observe
a minuet in the sky
transformation
ethereal shape shifters
dispersing with our attention
do they watch us too
dreamers lost in time
soaring high
blowing kisses in the wind

little girl lost

hey little girl
where are you going
daydreaming of
magic and wizards
residing in your imagination
can you see in the distance
a portal to another time

hey little girl
carrying rubies and gold in your bag
blowing out the candles on your cake
conjuring princess dresses with your mind
can you see the empty universe
ready for design

hey little girl
stepping over the rubble
grazed
the gravel sticking to your skin
shake it off
take my hand
I am with you
don't be scared
diamond armour protects us

boxes

Three silver boxes stored under her bed
souvenirs from another world
treasured and precious
polished with mortality

a box for yesterday
mementos overflowing
violets and sunshine
spilling onto the floor
she bathes in the perfumed light
a mosaic of broken glass

a box for today
crystalline garden in bloom
dew drops fall onto her tongue
a monkey and a tiger by her side
as she skips through the lushness
humming

an empty box for tomorrow
her favourite

refractions

accustomed to the road
on auto pilot
white light bends through the air
it redirects me to a new path
passing through the atmosphere
now free falling
the velocity makes me nervous
stop
who will catch me
I land in a ghost town
the wind plays hopscotch
with the tumbleweeds
I want to join them in their carefree games
but there is a new route to follow
carried high through the air currents
wild and free
reminds me to keep playing
transparent but I can see
the colours of the spectrum
navigating me to the exit
a slow descent back to the ground

ode to my ugg boots

an icon of my youth
how could I have forgotten you
constant through my adolescence
trusty accomplice to my shenanigans
grey beauty
discarded

unexpectedly
retuning into my thoughts
during lockdown
when uncertainty prevailed
I craved your cosy comfort
wanting nothing more than
to have my feet encased
in your warmth again
to be reacquainted with you
it was time

a new pair
black adorned with pom poms
that familiar feeling
slipping into nostalgia
like coming home
wiggling my toes
against the sheepskin
not going anywhere
a satisfying come back

inferno

she awoke to find she could start fire with her hands
her touch could melt
purification and destruction at her fingertips

elemental power under her control
darkness no longer an enemy
protector of the hearth
her flames warming those around her

but volcanic fire burns deep inside
smouldering embers igniting
devouring her from within
now ablaze

as she burns
her hair sends sparks
up into the heavens
like a swarm of fireflies
ashes falling
eclipsing the earth
she rises
with a candle in her hand
lighting the way

life's not waiting

come on come on let's go
we can't lose any more time
I can see the blossoms falling

but I'm not ready my impatient friend

you need to get moving my dear
there's so much to do
what's keeping you

may we go tomorrow please
I'm stuck in a rut
hands are pulling me back in

no tomorrow is not an option
we need to go now
the shadows are shifting

I have too much to carry
my bags are heavy
full of seashells and sand

leave them behind
you don't need them
we will travel light
look the moon is waning now

please wait don't go without me
I don't want to go alone
my voice echoing in the void
and how will we get there

we won't get lost
following the river
watch it flow
it knows where to go
we just need to make a start
vamos

Vamos means let's go, come on in Spanish.

the tidal wave

standing on the sand
looking out at the horizon
seen in the distance
a wall of water approaching
gravitational interactions
surges towards me
do I run
frozen
I close my eyes
a sacrifice to the sea gods
I hold my breath
quietude
tumbling into stillness
a raindrop
surrendering
my footprints washed away
the ocean is mine

D = ST

how do I calculate
the distance to your heart
an impassable highway
to an uncertain destination
city lights up ahead
nearly there
roadblock
now unreachable
stops and starts
slams progress

speed and time
not in my hands
measuring our acceleration
moments pass
never ready
opposite rays
now off course drifting
hold on
keep going

philematology

lips barely touching
tentative
inching closer
the breeze whispers
hidden secrets into our ear
we listen
eyes closed in fusion
inhaling each other's soul
transcending to a different timeline
we are hushed by the sweetness
euphoria rushes in
flowing through our
delicate entanglement
a moment standing still
breaking the spell
a first kiss

untamed

a wild thing
she could not be domesticated
at home in the wilderness
making mud pies
playing with snails
watching their tentacles
withdraw when she touches them
studying how they feel
their way through life
leaving a gilded trail behind
daisy chain crown
and love beads around her neck
she dances with the rain
twirling
a symbiotic partner
conversing with the feral cats
reciting her memoirs
they understood her spirit
she wants to be the night sky
and have the stars join her for tea
skipping through the dawn
gathering stones
she finds along the way

everything will be ok

I remember now
frozen
uncertainty came knocking
I didn't want to answer
hiding under the covers
until it went way
pressing fast forward
to a different song
I longed to hear something else
to bypass what was playing

I remember now
the path had overgrown
couldn't see where it was going
had to slash it with my sword
looking up to the stairless tower
unconquerable
I needed wings to fly
but they had been clipped
I peeked through the keyhole
wanting to shout
but my voice was asleep
wake up
wake up
dismantling myself
a piece at a time
reassembled with an allen key

I remember now
tomorrow came out in the wash
and didn't leave a stain

wanderlust

through the darkness
I travelled through time
to find me
a quick tour stop
picked up pain
along the way
my luggage left behind
pilgrimage
with rhythm and light
filled my bags
with sunshine
landing in equanimity
I'll stay here for a while
new routes discovered
and territories explored
with a changing itinerary
visas required
sending postcards to you
I found a place
I'll go back to
the journey continues
I've got more pages to stamp

maze

I follow it
into the labyrinth
leaving crumbs
as it walked
offerings to an
unknown deity
in my hands
they turn to powder
on all fours
hungry and cold
the silence gets under
my fingernails
I search for the exit
trapped in the spiral
a new direction
with no way out

dusk calls the cicadas
to sing
I follow their song
to the centre
catching a glimpse
of it again
its shadow stayed with me
and took my hand
placed a star
above my head
pointing to the exit
a slow walk
through the
circuitous path
to knowingness
there it waits

www.ingramcontent.com/pod-product-compliance
Lightning Source LLC
Chambersburg PA
CBHW071039080526
44587CB00015B/2682